# CONFIRMATION

## PREPARING

## CELEBRATING

## REMEMBERING

*Text by*
FRANCES C. HEEREY, S.C.H.

**The Regina Press**
**New York**

# Introduction

Dear Candidate, Parents and Sponsors,

I address three categories of people in this letter of introduction because you are the primary people for whom this book has been written. In the mysterious designs of God, you are asked to participate in the initiation rites of a young person who will be received fully into the community of the Roman Catholic Church through the sacrament of Confirmation.

You, parents of the candidate, will see your role as significant Chrisitan witnesses take on a newer form. Although still under your protective care, the young person will begin to assume greater personal responsibility towards faith development and will share more actively and intelligently in your family and community events, in worship of God, and in care of the needy.

You, sponsor of the candidate will, during the preparation and celebration of the sacrament, represent the community's reception, support, and love for the candidate.

You, the CANDIDATE for the sacrament of Confirmation, will need to concentrate on an intelligent and prayerful preparation for this third step in your initiation rites in the Roman Catholic Church. The material in this book has been designed to help you and the Church community as you travel together on your faith journey. You took the first step on the journey at Baptism. You continued it with the second initiation step on the day of your First Holy Communion. The celebration of the sacrament of Confirmation is your third initial step on your faith journey.

From here on it will be up to you to continue this life-long journey hand-in-hand with Jesus, in praise of our Father, and with the strength of the Holy Spirit.

God's blessings be yours to the fullest!

SISTER FRANCES HEEREY, SCH

# MEMORY PRINT-OUT
## ON *YOU*

# PREPARING

Word processors, memory machines, and other computers are great helps in recalling data. Photographs are wonderful aids in remembering certain places and events in your life. The human memory is the best source for recalling feelings about God and people in your life. Knowledge and feelings are part of your growth and development as a unique person, one made in the image and likeness of God.

For a test case, come on a personal sacrament journey. Close your eyes. Let your memory work on the three past sacrament events in your faith-life.

## HOLY EUCHARIST (First Holy Communion)

Concentrate on the faces of the people who were present at your First Holy Communion:

YOU   PRIEST   PARENTS
TEACHERS   FRIENDS

Name those people who were present.

Describe your feelings about them during the event.

## RECONCILIATION (First Penance)

Concentrate on the faces of the people who were present at your First Confession:

YOU   PRIEST   PARENTS
TEACHERS   FRIENDS

Name those people who were present.

Describe your feelings about them during the event.

## BAPTISM

Concentrate on the faces of the people who were present at your Baptism. Photographs will help.

YOU   PRIEST   PARENTS
GOD-PARENTS   FAMILY   FRIENDS

Name those people who were present.

What are your feelings now about those people?

Your memories of people and your feelings during the three sacrament events, however vivid or dull, obviously support the fact that you are a member of a Christian people who celebrate sacrament events in faith. As you continue your sacrament journey (Holy Orders, Marriage, Anointing of the Sick, Confirmation), you will become more aware of God and of the important people who travel along life's journey with you. These people form your Church community. Together you are followers of Jesus Christ, true God and true man.

So, what has been in it for you to date? Well, you have been the center of attention in your community. You are engaged in a process, a beginning of a life-long event. You are being initiated into a Christian community, the Catholic Church, whose life and center is Jesus Christ.

*YOU* entered into the Church community through *Baptism*. If ever you break relationship with God and members of the community through sin, you are restored to their friendship through *Penance*. Each day Jesus gives you His generous love and forgiveness through *Holy Eucharist*.

Through your reflections and remembrances you will gradually understand that you are a child of God with a special mission in life to follow and imitate Jesus. Your community is assisting you in your initiation rules into full membership.

# CELEBRATING

Yahweh, you examine me and know me,
You know if I am standing or sitting,
You read my thoughts from afar,
whether I walk or lie down, you are watching,
You know every detail of my conduct.

The word is not even on my tongue,
Yahweh, before you know all about it;
close behind and close in front you fence me round,
shielding me with your hand.
Such knowledge is beyond my understanding,
a height to which my mind cannot attain.

Where could I go to escape your spirit?
Where could I flee from your presence?
If I climb the heaven, you are there,
there too, if I lie in sheol.

If I flew to the point of sunrise,
or westward across the sea,
Your hand will still be guiding me,
your right hand holding me.

It was you who created my inmost self
and put me together in my mother's womb;
for all these mysteries I thank you:
for the wonder of myself, for the wonder of your
    works.

PSALM 139 (v. 1-10, 13-14)

# REMEMBERING

1. **Who made me?**

   Out of his infinite love for me, God made me in His own image and likeness.

2. **What is the mission God has given me in life?**

   God has entrusted to me the mission to witness by word and deed to the love of God for all creation.

3. **In what do I resemble God?**

   God created me with an immortal soul in which resides the powers of understanding and free will. Becuase my soul is immortal, it will never die.

4. **What help does God give me to fulfill my mission?**

   God gives me the Holy Spirit, the Roman Catholic Church community, the sacraments and worship, Scripture, and other good people.

5. **When did I become a member of the Roman Catholic Community?**

   I became a member of the Roman Catholic community at my Baptism. I received a fuller membership at the sacrament of Holy Eucharist. The final initiation rite will take place at the sacrament of Confirmation.

# SCRIPTURE

# PREPARING

If you are an attentive reader, and a good listener, you will like the Bible. What's in this book for you? Well, the Bible, also known as Sacred Scripture, is a print-out of the prophetic events which told of the coming of the Messiah (Old Testament); and of the life, death, resurrection, and ascension of that Messiah Who is Jesus (New Testament). In this book you will discover that Jesus is for you.

The two divisions of the Bible are the Old Testament and the New Testament. They contain a variety of writing styles to convey the convincing message that God loves us. The styles are: historical accounts of the chosen people and the people of God, poetry, psalms (music), parables, and letters. The historical period begins with the accounts of creation, carries through the covenants that God made with His chosen people, and through the life of Jesus and His early Church.

In conveying the message and mystery of God's love for all creation, the Biblical writers often used *images* readily accessible to the people, such as water, light, rock, wind, salt, death, and life. For instance, we read in the Psalms: Oh God, you are my rock, my stronghold.

There are also many *themes* found in the Bible: love, forgiveness, fasting, peace, covenant, life, justice, liberation, Messiah, resurrection, hope, and witness. The parables of Jesus are filled with themes. Remember the story of the Prodigal Son? Forgiveness and love are the themes.

The Bible is a source of inspiration and prayer. It should be read with great reverence because it is the Word of God.

## THE BIBLE BRINGS GOD TO US AND US TO GOD.

Loving the Bible is one sure way to know much about Jesus and His love for you.

# CELEBRATING

The Word of God is not fossilized but alive. It is vibrant. For centuries visual and audio artists have taken men and women in the Scriptures and portrayed them in memorable style. Today you can hear rock and country-western artists, captivated especially with Jesus and the love of God, singing their Gospel creations. At Easter and Christmas, the world prayerfully celebrates Handel's 18th Century composition, ''The Messiah.'' Think of the master artists' creations on Christmas cards which you see each winter season.

And you? How can you creatively use your talents to celebrate the Scriptures? Think about the possibilities of doing something now. Use one of the following medium for your personal expression.

POETRY  PAINTING  MUSIC  SCULPTURE
DRAMA  VIDEO TAPE  PRAYER

Whatever manner you choose to celebrate the Bible, remember to begin by giving the Bible a special place of honor in your home or your room. Read it frequently. Pray it daily.

REMEMBER THAT
THE BIBLE BRINGS GOD TO US
AND US TO GOD.

# REMEMBERING

1. **What is the Bible?**

   Also known as Sacred Scripture, the Bible is the inspired Word of God. It is divided into the Old Testament and the New Testament.

2. **What is the main message of the Bible?**

   The main message of the Bible is that God loves us.

3. **Name the four general divisions of the Old Testament.**

   The four general divisions of the Old Testament are: the Pentateuch, the Historical Books, the Poetical and Wisdom Books, and the Prophetical Books.

   These books give an account of God's love and actions in the lives of His people, preparing them for the coming of Jesus the Messiah.

4. **Name the general divisions of the New Testament.**

   The general divisions of the New Testament are: 4 Gospels, 21 Epistles, the Acts of the Apostles, and the Book of Revelation.

   The materials in these divisions relate the life, death, resurrection, ascension, and the teachings of Jesus, the promised Messiah.

5. **What are some themes found in the Bible?**

   Some themes found in the Bible are love, for-giveness, fasting, justice, covenant, life, libera-tion, messiah, resurrection, hope, and witness.

6. **What techniques do some of the Biblical writers use to convey the message and mystery of God?**

   The Biblical writers sometimes used imagery to convey the message and mystery of God. Some images used are water, light, rock, wind, salt, life and death.

7. **How should the Bible be read?**

   Since the Bible is a source of inspiration and prayer, it should be read with great reverence.

# MORALITY

# PREPARING

You have probably heard the popular expression, "I'm OK; You're OK." What does it mean to you? For the faith-filled Christian who sees the expression in the light of the values of Jesus (honesty, selflessness, service), it means that persons who truly witness to Jesus always feel good about themselves. In fact, the hardened criminal, the liar, the person who stole your bicycle, is really not so bad. Those people are "OK," too, because Jesus' virtue of forgiveness strangely makes it that way.

Jesus' actions and lifestyle were based on the Mosaic law, the 10 Commandments. He expanded the understanding of these commandments by placing them into two simple teachings:

**This is the first:**

Hear, O Israel! The Lord our God is Lord alone! Therefore, you shall love the Lord your God with all your heart, You shall love the Lord your God with all your soul, You shall love the Lord your God with all your mind, You shall love the Lord your God with all your strength.

**This is the second:**

You shall love your neighbor as yourself.

MARK 12:28

Jesus' value system is found chiefly in the 8 Beatitudes. Look at the Beatitudes on the following

21

pages. Discover the positive attitudes which Jesus promoted. If your attitudes are good, your actions will be good, too. This basically is the foundation of a Christian conscience. The Holy Spirit is the true source of strength to do good actions. This is what Christian morality is all about.

There are times when "I'm OK; You're OK" becomes a negative, "I'm not OK; therefore, you are not OK!" This happens when you have let yourself down; when you succumb to selfishness and laziness, or if you become involved in a drug/alcohol abuse scene. Community members suffer from your breaks in relationship with them them.

It is then that the invitation to restore your sense of "OK-ness" is offered by God, who even in your sin wants you to share more deeply in His love. God says, "Confess your sins. Repent, and you will rejoice!" Once you experience God's mercy, you show mercy to others.

Assuming responsibility for God's law of love requires keeping up on and doing something about the many moral issues which face society. These issues include: respect for all life (unborn, handicapped, aged), racial prejudice, poverty, housing, and the hungry.

Living Christian morality to its fullest can bring Jesus to you. In the light of all you have just read, picture His smiling face as Jesus says to *You*,

"I'm OK. You're OK."

# CELEBRATING

## The Beatitudes

How happy are the poor in spirit:
   theirs is the kingdom of heaven.

Happy the gentle:
   they shall have the earth for their heritage.

Happy those who mourn:
   they shall be comforted.

Happy those who hunger and thirst for what is
      right:
   they shall be satisfied.

Happy the merciful:
   they shall have mercy shown them.

Happy the pure in heart:
   they shall see God.

Happy the peacemakers:
   they shall be called the children of God.

Happy those who are persecuted in the cause of
      right:
   theirs is the kingdom of heaven.

**1. What is Christian morality?**

Christian morality is a system of values based on the life and teachings of Jesus.

**2. What are some important values Jesus taught us?**

Jesus taught us honesty, selflessness, service and respect for all life.

**3. What did Jesus base His lifestyle on?**

Jesus based His lifestyle and actions on the 10 Commandments and God's law of love.

**4. What are the 8 Beatitudes?**

These are the lessons on real happiness which Jesus gave His people. They are the foundation for a good Christian conscience.

**5. Who is the source of strength to do good actions?**

The Holy Spirit is the source of strength to do good actions.

**6. What is conscience?**

Conscience is my ability to make a moral judgment. It is my consciousness of God's will for me.

### 7. How do I form my conscience?

I form my conscience by praying, listening to God, and taking on the attitudes of Jesus.

### 8. What is sin?

Sin is first a deliberate offense against God's law of love. It is a failure to respond to God's love, to serve my neighbor, to respond to what my conscience tells me.

### 9. What are the kinds of sin?

Sin is divided into: mortal and venial.

### 10. What is venial sin?

Venial sin is a deliberate break in relationship with God and others.

### 11. What are the criteria for determining mortal sin?

The criteria for determining mortal sin are: the sin must be grave; there must be full awareness of the grave sin; there must be full freedom to commit the offence.

### 12. What is original sin?

Original sin is the first break in relationship of human beings with God. Every person is born with original sin and with its consequences (ignorance, pain, and death). Baptism takes away original sin.

# PREPARING

What do these lists have in common?

|   | I | II | III |
|---|---|---|---|
| A. | Rock Stars<br>Entertainers<br>People Who Care | Live Aid Concert<br>Farm Aid Concert<br>Benefit Dinners | Starving Africans<br>American Farmers<br>Education for Poor |
| B. | Missionaries<br>Holy Childhood<br>Catholic Relief<br>Services | Mission Appeals<br>Lenten Boxes<br>Money<br>Food Collections<br>Clothing | Global Villagers<br>Starving Children<br>Lebanese Refugees<br>Third World<br>Refugees |
| C. | Caring Christian<br>Community<br>School Service<br>Clubs<br>Parish Youth<br>Organizations | Meals-on-Wheels<br>Marathons<br>Dances | Shut-Ins<br>Handicapped<br>Drug/Alcohol<br>Abusers |

Television specials, newspapers, magazines and popular songs bring you the needs of the poor of the global village. Can you count the number of times you have sung, ''We Are the World,'' or heard the theme from ''Hands Across America''? Didn't you really feel part of it all?

Besides the devastating effects of drought, fire and floods, human life is, unfortunately, destroyed in many other ways, e.g., abortion, fetal experimentation, euthanasia, and dignity destroying medicines. Human life is diminished in many ways (violence, drugs, child abuse, prejudice, loneliness, rejection, physical and mental handicaps).

The Gospel of Jesus calls us to make our world safe for all people. The above mentioned groups, causes, and activities help to deepen our awareness of the Christian community as servant in the world. They help us realize the great teaching of Jesus to respect all life.

As you grow in love of God and other people whom the Lord sends into your daily life, you will begin to assume greater responsibility in caring. Not only your family but members of your faith community and the global village will benefit from your goodness. The power of the Holy Spirit will startle you at times, particularly when you wonder how you ever made the time to do that good deed. It is all a beginning, part of the awakenings to the real meaning of initiation rites.

Christian social concern is based on commitment to the Gospel. Leadership for you will be found in the Catholic Church. Present and past Popes always taken strong stands on social concerns. Bishops set forth the teachings of Jesus and the Catholic Church in pastoral letters. Sisters, brothers, deacons, priests and other generous people, like members of your Christian community, give unselfishly of time and energy to witness to the love of God for all people.

# CELEBRATING

Oh, how I love you, Jesus
My heart is racing to keep pace with you.
You gave me new life
In *Baptismal* rite
Through water and power of spirit.

Oh, how I thank you, Jesus,
For *Eucharist*: Body and Blood and Word.
For strength on life's journey
The food to support me
That joins me to you and to others.

Oh, how I marvel, Jesus
Each time that you give me *forgiveness* and love
When sometimes I'm selfish
And forget to serve others.
You restore all by giving me *Peace*.

Oh, how I need you, Jesus
My heart needs healing with Your Holy Spirit.
With compassion and zeal
For a world in great need
of respect for all life done in *Justice*.

# REMEMBERING

**1. What does the Gospel of Jesus call us to do?**

The Gospel of Jesus calls us 1) to respect all life (including unborn, handicapped, aged); 2) to make our world safe for all people.

**2. How can human life be destroyed?**

Human life is destroyed by selfish acts, such as abortion, fetal experimentation, euthanasia, the use of dignity destroying medicines, drug and alcohol abuse, and physical and mental violence.

**3. Whose lives are you asked to care for?**

I am asked to care for my own life, the lives of my family and community members and the whole global village.

**4. Who gives me strength to care for myself and other people?**

The Holy Spirit will always give me strength to do good works.

## 5. Where can I find assistance in knowing how to care for others?

Leadership to help me care for others is given by the Pope, bishops, sisters, brothers, deacons, priests and committed members of the Christian community.

# BASIC TEACHINGS

# PREPARING

"Gift" and "talent" are challenging and intriguing words. Perhaps in the clubs or organizations you belong to you have had the opportunity to discover and use your gifts and talents for the good of others. A well-run organization provides handbooks of rules and teachings so that the members may intelligently participate in its life and activities.

Usually a period of initiation studies and rites take place before full membership is given to a candidate for any club.

As a community of believers, the Catholic Church has its official guidelines on the teachings of Jesus. You have been learning about them and have been personally involved in them since your Baptism. The basic teachings help you to know, love, and serve God and people in need. They help you to do so intelligently, with a spirit of justice, and in the great peace that Jesus gives to His followers. They prompt you to recognize your gifts and talents. The Holy Spirit gives you the power to use the gifts and talents fully.

As you prepare for the Sacrament of Confirmation, you should review carefully the basic teachings of the Church. The basic teachings concern God, (Father, Son, Holy Spirit), Church, Mary and the Saints, Morality, Scripture, Worship/Sacraments.

The Bishops will ask you during the celebration of the sacrament of Confirmation if you believe in the holy Catholic Church. Know what you mean when you answer, ''I do.''

The following pages give a summary of the basic teachings of the Roman Catholic Church.

# CELEBRATING

There are many ways of celebrating, aren't there? You can throw a party, fly a kite, make a cake, invite friends over to your house. We know that Jesus celebrated often with his family and friends. In John 2 we read of Jesus attending a wedding in Cana. To help the young couple out of an embarassing situation, Jesus increased their supply of refreshments.

How can you celebrate something like *basic teachings*? How have other people celebrated them? In his enthusiasm for all creation, St. Francis of Assisi constantly called upon all creatures to praise God. He once said to a cricket, ''Sing, Sister Cricket, and praise the Lord with joyful tones.'' St. Frances Cabrini celebrated God's love up to the minute of her death. After bagging the orphans' Christmas candy, Frances sat in her chair and quietly slipped off to her Creator. St. Thomas Aquinas, a brilliant scholar, spent his life trying to explain in great volumes the mysteries of God. When she was a young teenager, Elizabeth Ann Seton brought food, clothing and medicine to poor people in New York City.

The secret of celebration of the basic teachings seems to be mirroring the love of God in your life. What will be your style of celebration?

# REMEMBERING

*God   Jesus   Church   Mary/Saints   Prayer*

## GOD

**1. Who is God?**

God is the Supreme Being.

**2. How many Persons are there in God?**

There are 3 Persons in God: Father, Son, and Holy Spirit. These 3 Persons form a community bound together in love. This mystery is known as the Blessed Trinity.

**3. Which Scripture reference tells of the Blessed Trinity?**

When Jesus was baptized, "Heaven opened and the Holy Spirit descended on him in bodily shape, like a dove. And a voice came from heaven, 'You are my Son, the Beloved.'" (Luke 3:22)

**4. What are the ways in which you can know the love of God?**

You can know the love of God by
1) growing in self-awareness and self-acceptance with a great capacity for an authentic love of others.

2) experiencing faith as a personal relationship with God.
3) developing a conscious spiritual life, a sense of community, and membership in the Catholic community.

## GOD THE FATHER

**1. Who is the Father?**

The Father is God and the First Person of the Blessed Trinity.

**2. What was the main work of the Father?**

By a free and hidden plan of His own wisdom and goodness, the eternal Father created the whole universe.

## JESUS, GOD THE SON

**1. Who is Jesus Christ?**

Jesus Christ is God, and the Second Person of the Blessed Trinity. Jesus is both God and man.

**2. How do we know that Jesus was the promised Messiah?**

We know that Jesus was the promised Messiah because everything that the prophets in the Old Testament had foretold of Him were fulfilled.

### 3. What was Jesus' main work on earth?

Through His life, prophecies, miracles, death and resurrection, Jesus showed us the love of God the Father and the power of the Holy Spirit. He won for us our redemption through forgiveness of our sins. He promised us true happiness with Him in heaven.

### 4. What does the resurrection of Jesus prove to us?

The resurrection of Jesus proved that Jesus is the Son of God.

### 5. What happened to Jesus on Good Friday and Easter Sunday?

Jesus died on the Cross on Good Friday. He rose from the dead on Easter Sunday.

### 6. What is the feast of the Ascension?

On the feast of the Ascension we celebrate the day that Jesus returned body, soul and spirit to His Father in heaven.

### 7. How can we best follow Jesus?

We can follow Jesus by loving and worshiping God our Father, by continuing His works of justice, peace, and mercy on behalf of any person in need.

### 8. How is Jesus present to His Church?

Jesus is present to His Church through the Holy Spirit. He acts through the seven sacraments.

## GOD THE HOLY SPIRIT

**1. Who is the Holy Spirit?**

The Holy Spirit is God and the Third Person of the Blessed Trinity.

**2. When did the Holy Spirit first descend upon the Apostles?**

The Holy Spirit first descended upon the Apostles on the day of Pentecost.

**3. When did you first receive the Holy Spirit in your soul?**

I first received the Holy Spirit on the event of my Baptism.

**4. What are the gifts of the Holy Spirit?**

The gifts of the Holy Spirit are wisdom, understanding, counsel, fortitude, patience, knowledge, piety, and fear of the Lord.

**5. What does the Holy Spirit do for you?**

The Holy Spirit empowers and obliges me to be a witness to Jesus.

## THE CHURCH

**1. What is the Church?**

The Church is the community of believers called to give glory and praise to the Father and to bring God's redeeming love to all His people.

## 2. What is the mission of the Church?

The mission of the Church is to continue the work of Jesus.

## 3. What does membership in the Church require?

Membership in the Church requires faith and baptism, active participation in its life, worship, works of mercy, sacramental events, and obedience to all its laws.

## 4. What are the laws of the Church?

1. To keep holy the day of the Lord's resurrection.
2. To receive Holy Communion frequently and the Sacrament of Reconciliation regularly.
3. To study Catholic teaching.
4. To observe the Marriage laws of the Church.
5. To strengthen and support the Church.
6. To do penance.
7. To join in the missionary spirit of the Church.

## 5. What does membership in the Church community mean for me?

Membership in the Church community means concern for all human life within the community; service to people experiencing racial prejudice, exploitation, discrimination, and all other forms of injustice.

## 6. Where are the social teachings of the Church found?

The social teachings of the Church are found in documents written by popes and bishops. All writings are based on the teachings of Jesus.

# MARY AND THE SAINTS

**1. Who is the Blessed Virgin Mary?**

The Blessed Virgin Mary is the Mother of Jesus, the Mother of God, and our Mother.

**2. What is meant by Mary's Immaculate Conception?**

Mary's Immaculate Conception means that she was the only person created by God who was preserved from original sin. (This is celebrated on December 8th.)

**3. What was the Feast of Mary's Assumption?**

The Feast of Mary's Assumption celebrates the occasion when Mary's body, soul and spirit were brought directly into heaven. (This is celebrated on August 15th.)

**4. Why do we call Mary our Mother?**

When Jesus was dying on the Cross He gave Mary to us as our Mother when He said to the Apostle John, ''Son, behold your Mother.''

**5. Who belongs to the Communion of Saints?**

To the Communion of Saints belong:
1. people who mirror God in their lives
2. souls in purgatory
3. saints in heaven.

**6. Why do we venerate the saints?**

We venerate the saints because they imitated Jesus in their lives by loving and serving God and people in need.

# LITURGY AND SACRAMENTS

# PREPARING

You do pray, don't you? When, where, and how you pray depends upon circumstances and reasons for prayer. Sometimes you are alone with the Lord; other times you are with people and the Lord. Prayer brings you closer to God and to other people.

What's in it for you? The Christian community believes that one of the most effective prayers is the Church's liturgy. Actually, the liturgy is the official prayer of the community of believers. Remember, Jesus promised that where two or three are gathered in His name, He is there, too? So, when the community gathers for public prayer, Jesus is right there, praying with us and for us. Jesus is with us sharing his thoughts, moods, and interests.

In the liturgy, Jesus comes to us exactly where we are. He brings us to our Father, with great warmth and love. The liturgical events in the community are primarily the celebration of the seven sacraments and praying of the Divine Office.

To date, you have celebrated: the initiation sacraments of Baptism and the Eucharist; the healing sacrament of Reconciliation. You continue to celebrate the Eucharist each time you attend Mass and receive Holy Communion. Confirmation, like Baptism and the Eucharist, is an initiation sacrament. The sacrament of Reconciliation (Penance) can be a weekly or monthly event. The other healing sacrament is the Anointing of the Sick. The celebration of the Anointing of the Sick is an occasional event which brings the community together to pray and care for the sick or elderly. Marriage and Holy Orders are sometimes referred to as the vocational sacraments. Marriage and Holy Orders are sacraments in which people dedicate themselves to live a special calling of holiness in the Church.

It takes faith to see what is in it for you each time you celebrate a sacrament or pray in your private place.

# CELEBRATING

What's in it for me,
This being part of community
   of believers
   who worship
   with others?

Try it.

Subtlety, gradually
The question becomes
Who's in it for me?

And the winning response is

    JESUS

In thought, interest, and mood.

# REMEMBERING

### 1. How does Jesus act in the Church?

Jesus acts through the seven sacraments. Through them, God is worshiped and people are made holy.

### 2. What is a sacrament?

A sacrament is a sign of God's presence in the world. The sacraments give grace.

### 3. What is grace?

Grace is the free gift of God Himself to His people.

### 4. Name the seven sacraments.

The seven sacraments are: Baptism, Eucharist, Confirmation, Reconciliation, Anointing of the Sick, Matrimony, and Holy Orders.

### 5. What is Baptism?

Through the sacrament of Baptism, Jesus unites me with His death and resurrection, joins me to His Body, the Church, and gives me a share in God's life (grace). It, thereby, takes away original sin.

### 6. What is Holy Eucharist?

The Holy Eucharist is the sacrament of the Body and Blood of Jesus Christ. Jesus gathers

His people together to worship the Father and to celebrate His own death and resurrection.

## 7. What is Confirmation?

Through the Sacrament of Confirmation, Jesus confers on Christians the seal of the Holy Spirit, empowering and obliging them to be His witnesses.

## 8. What is Reconciliation?

Through the Sacrament of Reconciliation, Jesus forgives my sins, restores and strengthens my relationship with the Father and members of the community.

## 9. What is the Anointing of the Sick?

Through the Sacrament of the Anointing of the Sick, Jesus and members of the Church community show their love and concern for those members who are seriously sick or aged.

## 10. What is Holy Orders?

Through the Sacrament of Holy Orders, Jesus calls certain members of the community (deacons, priests, bishops) to serve God's people. He empowers them to preach His Word and to celebrate the sacraments with the community.

## 11. What is matrimony?

Matrimony is the sacrament whereby Jesus is present with the Church to celebrate and bless the union of man and woman.

# CONFIRMATION

# PREPARING

## The Special Sacrament Event
## on Your Present Journey

### CONFIRMATION

And now you have arrived at another sacrament event on your personal sacrament journey. The sacrament of Confirmation, which will be your third initiation sacrament, will be a new source of grace and strength for you. You will be sealed with the Holy Spirit. Jesus is the reason.

Once received, the sacrament of Confirmation will enable you to profess publicly the name of Jesus and to be a witness to His life, death, and resurrection. It is another *beginning* step in becoming an active member of the community of believers which is the Body of Christ. Simply put it means you will try to follow Jesus in His way of love, justice, and peace.

How can you do this?

THROUGH THE HOLY SPIRIT

WHOSE POWER WILL ASSIST YOU —

to follow Jesus whenever He calls (CALL)

to care for people in need (CONVERSION)

49

to stand up for Him and His people
    (COMMITMENT)
to respond in a responsible manner to Jesus' calls
    (CHALLENGE)

The ordinary minister of the sacrament of Confirmation is the Bishop. The Bishop is the chief teacher in the diocese and he is responsible to help you develop your faith-life as you follow Jesus.

During the celebration of the sacrament of Confirmation the Bishop will call upon the Holy Spirit to be your helper and guide. He does this as he places his hands over your head. The Bishop will make the sign of the cross with chrism on your forehead. (Chrism is a mixture of olive oil and balm.) The Bishop will say, ''_____'' (your confirmation name), be sealed with the Holy Spirit.

Once that rite occurs, the Holy Spirit will have entered your soul in a mysterious and deeper way. You will have finished your initiation rites. These rites give you formal entrance into the Christian Community, the Roman Catholic Church. The occasion will be one of great rejoicing for you and for the community.

Remember: a witness is one who stands up and is noticed!

# CELEBRATING

## The Rite of Confirmation

In performing the simple ceremony, which ordinarily takes place during the Liturgy of the Eucharist, the Bishop

1. imposed his hands over the candidate.
2. calls upon the Holy Spirit to be the person's helper and guide.
3. makes the sign of the cross with chrism on the candidate's forehead.
4. says, ''_____'' (name), be sealed with the Holy Spirit.

While the Bishop is confirming the candidate, a sponsor places a hand on the candidate's shoulder. The sponsor encourages the confirmed Christian to be a true witness of Jesus Christ. The sponsor does this on behalf of the whole Christian community.

(Before the actual rite of the sacrament takes place, the Bishop will present the teachings of the Catholic Church and he will encourage the candidate to continue well on the journey of faith. He will ask the candidate to renew baptismal vows. This is a series of five questions to which the candidate responds, ''I do.''

1. **What is the sacrament of Confirmation?**

   The sacrament of Confirmation is a sacrament of initiation. Through this sacrament Jesus confers on Christians the seal of the Holy Spirit, empowering and obliging them to be His witnesses.

2. **What two essential elements compose the sacrament of Confirmation?**

   The sacrament of Confirmation is composed of matter and form.

3. **What is the matter of Confirmation?**

   The matter of the sacrament of Confirmation is the imposition of the hands of the Bishop. He calls upon the Holy Spirit to be the person's helper and guide. He makes the sign of the cross with chrism on the person's forehead.

4. **What is the form of Confirmation?**

   The form of the sacrament is the Bishop's statement: ''_____ (name), be sealed with the Holy Spirit.''

5.  **What is the role of the sponsor in the sacrament of Confirmation?**

    The sponsor acts on behalf of the whole Christian community which encourages the confirmed Christian to fulfill the promise to be a true witness of Jesus Christ.

6.  **What two sacrament events are integrally connected with Confirmation?**

    Confirmation is one of the three sacraments of *initiation*: Baptism, Confirmation, and Eucharist.

7.  **When is the sacrament of Confirmation ordinarily celebrated?**

    The sacrament of Confirmation is ordinarily celebrated during the Liturgy of the Eucharist.

# PRAYERS AND DEVOTIONS

# Special Prayers
# That We Should Know

## THE OUR FATHER

Our Father who art in heaven, hallowed be thy name. Thy kingdom come. Thy will be done on earth as it is in heaven. Give us this day our daily bread and forgive us our trespasses as we forgive those who trespass against us and lead us not into temptation, but deliver us from evil.   Amen.

## THE HAIL MARY

Hail Mary full of grace the Lord is with Thee. Blessed art thou among women and blessed is the fruit of thy womb Jesus. Holy Mary Mother of God pray for us sinners now and at the hour of our death.   Amen.

## GLORY BE TO THE FATHER

Glory be to the Father and to the Son and to the Holy Spirit, as it was in the beginning is now and ever shall be world without end.   Amen.

## AN ACT OF CONTRITION

O my God I am heartily sorry for having offended Thee and I detest all my sins because of Thy just punishment, but most of all because they offend Thee, my God, Who are all good, and deserving of all my love. I firmly resolve with the help of Thy grace, to sin no more, and to avoid the near occasions of sin.   Amen.

## THE APOSTLES CREED

I believe in God, the Father Almighty, Creator of heaven and earth; and in Jesus Christ, His only Son, our Lord; who was conceived by the Holy Spirit, born of the Virgin Mary, suffered under Pontius Pilate, was crucified, died and was buried.

He descended into hell; the third day He arose again from the dead. He ascended into heaven, sits at the right hand of God, the Father Almighty; thence He shall come to judge the living and the dead. I believe in the Holy Spirit, the Holy Catholic Church, the communion of saints, the forgiveness of sins, the resurrection of the body and life everlasting.   Amen.

# PRAYER TO THE HOLY SPIRIT

Come, O Holy Spirit, fill the hearts of Your faithful and kindle in them the fire of Your love.

V. Send forth Your Spirit and they shall be created.

R. And You shall renew the face of the earth.

*Let us pray:*

O God, who has taught the hearts of the faithful by the light of the Holy Spirit, grant that in the same Spirit, we may be always truly wise and ever rejoice in His consolation. Through Christ our Lord. Amen.

# BLESSING BEFORE MEALS

Bless us, Lord, and these Thy gifts which we are about to receive from Thy bountiful hands, through Christ our Lord. Amen.

# GRACE AFTER MEALS

We give Thee thanks, Almighty God, for these Thy gifts through Christ our Lord. Amen.

## THE ''MEMORARE''

Remember, O most gracious Virgin Mary, that never was it known that anyone who fled to your protection, implored your help or sought your intercession, was left unaided. Inspired with this confidence, I fly to you, O Virgin of virgins, my Mother; to you do I come, before you I stand, sinful and sorrowful. O Mother of the Word Incarnate, despise not my petitions, but in your mercy hear and answer me.   Amen.

## ACT OF FAITH

O my God, I believe that you are one God in three Divine Persons: Father, Son and Holy Spirit. I believe that Your Divine Son became Man and died for our sins, and that He will come again to judge the living and the dead. I believe these and all the truths that the Catholic Church teaches, because You have revealed them, who can neither deceive nor be deceived.   Amen.

## ACT OF HOPE

O my God, relying on Your almighty power and infinite mercy and promises, I hope to obtain pardon of my sins, the help of Your grace and life everlasting through the merits of Jesus Christ, my Lord and Redeemer.   Amen.

## ACT OF LOVE

O my God, I love you above all things with my whole heart and soul, because You are all good and worthy of all my love. I love my neighbor as myself for the love of You. I forgive all who have injured me and ask pardon of all whom I have injured. Amen.

# CHRISTIAN DOCTRINE

# SACRAMENTS

BAPTISM

CONFIRMATION

EUCHARIST

RECONCILIATION

ANOINTING OF THE SICK

MARRIAGE

HOLY ORDERS

# THE BEATITUDES

1. Blessed are the poor in spirit: the reign of God is theirs.

2. Blessed are the sorrowing: they shall be consoled.

3. Blessed are the lowly: they shall inherit the land.

4. Blessed are they who hunger and thirst for holiness: they shall have their fill.

5. Blessed are they who show mercy: mercy shall be theirs.

6. Blessed are the single-hearted: for they shall see God.

7. Blessed are the peacemakers: they shall be called sons of God.

8. Blessed are those persecuted for holiness' sake: the reign of God is theirs.

# THE WORKS OF MERCY

## THE CORPORAL WORKS OF MERCY

To feed the hungry.

To give drink to the thirsty.

To clothe the naked.

To visit and ransom the captives.

To shelter the homeless.

To visit the sick.

To bury the dead.

## THE SPIRITUAL WORKS OF MERCY

To admonish sinners.

To instruct the ignorant.

To counsel the doubtful.

To comfort the sorrowful.

To bear wrongs patiently.

To forgive all injuries.

To pray for the living and the dead.

# COMMANDMENTS OF GOD

## THE TEN COMMANDMENTS OF GOD

1 . I, the Lord, am your God. You shall not have strange gods besides me.
2. You shall not take the name of the Lord God in vain.
3. Remember to keep holy the Sabbath.
4. Honor your father and mother.
5. You shall not kill.
6. You shall not commit adultery.
7. You shall not steal.
8. You shall not bear false witness against your neighbor.
9. You shall not covet your neighbor's wife.
10. You shall not covet your neighbor's goods.

## COMMANDMENTS OF THE CHURCH

1. To keep holy the day of the Lord's resurrection.
2. To receive Holy Communion frequently and the Sacrament of Reconciliation regularly.
3. To study Catholic teaching.
4. To observe the marriage laws of the Church.
5. To strengthen and support the Church.
6. To do penance.
7. To join in the missionary spirit of the Church.

# DEVOTIONS

# STATIONS OF THE CROSS

*This is a prayer said during Lent. Many people say it all year round. There are fourteen stations.*

*Prayer*

Jesus, I want to be sorry for my sins. Help me to see how you suffered and died for me. Help me to know your mercy and forgiveness. Teach me how to say ''Thank You.''

+
1. JESUS IS CONDEMNED TO DIE

+
2. JESUS CARRIES HIS CROSS

+
3. JESUS FALLS THE FIRST TIME

+
4. JESUS MEETS HIS MOTHER MARY

+
5. SIMON HELPS JESUS

+
6. VERONICA WIPES JESUS' FACE

+

7. JESUS FALLS A SECOND TIME

+

8. JESUS MEETS THE WOMEN

+

9. JESUS FALLS THE THIRD TIME

+

10. JESUS IS STRIPPED OF HIS CLOTHES

+

11. JESUS IS NAILED TO THE CROSS

+

12. JESUS DIES

+

13. JESUS IS TAKEN DOWN

+

14. JESUS IS LAID IN THE TOMB

# THE ROSARY

The rosary is a special way of praying to God that honors Mary, the Mother of Jesus. While reciting prayers, you think about certain stories in the lives of Jesus and Mary. These stories are called mysteries: a mystery is a story about God.

Rosary beads are used to keep count of the prayers and mysteries. Recite the Apostles' Creed while you hold the crucifix, then one Our Father and three Hail Marys. After that, as you think about each mystery, recite the Our Father on the large bead, the Hail Mary on each of ten smaller beads and finish with a Glory Be. That makes one decade. The complete rosary consists of five decades. There are three sets of mysteries and five stories in each set.

## The Joyful Mysteries

1. The Coming of Jesus is Announced
2. Mary Visits Elizabeth
3. Jesus is Born
4. Jesus is Presented to God
5. Jesus is Found in the Temple

## The Sorrowful Mysteries

1. Jesus' Agony in the Garden
2. Jesus is Whipped
3. Jesus is Crowned with Thorns
4. Jesus Carries His Cross
5. Jesus Dies on the Cross

## The Glorious Mysteries

1. Jesus Rises from His Tomb
2. Jesus Ascends to Heaven
3. The Holy Spirit Descends
4. Mary is Assumed into Heaven
5. Mary is Crowned in Heaven

# SEASONS OF THE CHURCH YEAR

The family of God likes to celebrate God all year round during the seasons of the Church year. The seasons are:

ADVENT — CHRISTMAS

LENT — EASTER

PENTECOST

ORDINARY TIME

## ADVENT

This is the time in which the community prepares for the celebration of Jesus' birthday. Advent is a happy time when we awaken our hearts by praying special prayers or by having an advent wreath or by burning a Mary candle.

Advent celebration is about four weeks long.

# CHRISTMAS

Christmas is the time when we celebrate the birthday of Jesus. It is a time of gift-giving to others. Giving gifts reminds us of the best gift of all which our Father in heaven gave to us: Jesus our brother.

During the Christmas season we remember Mary the Mother of God, the Holy Family, the Epiphany when the Magi visited Jesus. We celebrate Jesus as the Prince of Peace.

# LENT

Lent is the time in which the community prepares for the celebration of the death and resurrection of Jesus. It is a serious time when we look at Jesus' great care and love for us. We do penance for our sins and tell Jesus and each other "I am sorry. Please forgive me."

Jesus forgives us through His suffering and death on the Cross.

During Lent we get ready for the new life and joy of Easter.

# EASTER

Easter is the most wonderful time when we celebrate the Resurrection of Jesus. God raised Jesus from the dead. It is a time of great joy. It is the alleluia time!

Jesus brings new life to the world. Every Sunday we celebrate the feast of the Lord's Resurrection.

# PENTECOST

Forty days after Jesus was raised from the dead, He ascended into heaven where He is seated at the right hand of the Father.

Afterwards, His Mother Mary and the Disciples waited in prayer for the coming of the Holy Spirit. On the day of Pentecost they had all gathered together in one place. The Holy Spirit appeared before the Apostles in tongues of fire. He sent them out to preach to the whole world the good news of Jesus. He told them to proclaim that all who believe and are baptized shall be saved.

# ORDINARY TIME

This is the rest of the time during the year when we worship God, by celebrating the Resurrection of Jesus and by listening to stories about the life and teachings of Jesus.

**Jesus said,**

"I WILL BE WITH YOU ALL DAYS, EVEN UNTIL THE END OF TIME."

# INSPIRATIONAL QUOTES

If anyone loves me he will keep my word,
and my Father will love him,
and we shall come to him
and make our home with him.          JOHN 14:23

I am writing this, my children,
to stop you from sinning,
but if anyone should sin,
we have our advocate with the Father,
Jesus Christ, who is just;
he is the sacrifice that takes our sins away,
and not only ours,
but the whole world's.          1 JOHN 2:1

I want a laity . . . who know their creed so well that
they can give an account of it, who know so much
history that they can defend it.

JOHN CARDINAL NEWMAN

Be children of the Church.

ST. ELIZABETH ANN SETON

Lord to whom shall we go? You have the words of
eternal life?          JOHN 7:68